MAKING MODERN
MODEL AIRCRAFT

Ten superb models of the
advanced aircraft from di
aviation – military, comm
and space-age – with all th
instructions and details necessary for true
scale perfection.

Other books by PETER FAIRHURST

MAKING MODEL CARS
MAKING MODEL AEROPLANES
MAKING MODEL WARTIME VEHICLES
MAKING MODEL RACING CARS

All published by CAROUSEL BOOKS

MAKING MODEL MODERN AIRCRAFT

A CAROUSEL BOOK 0 552 54237 7

First published in Great Britain by Carousel Books

PRINTING HISTORY
Carousel edition published 1984

Carousel Books are published by
Transworld Publishers Ltd.,
Century House, 61–63 Uxbridge Road,
Ealing, London W5 5SA.

Made and printed in Great Britain by
Cox & Wyman Ltd., Reading, Berks.

MAKING MODERN
MODEL AIRCRAFT

Written and illustrated by
Peter Fairhurst

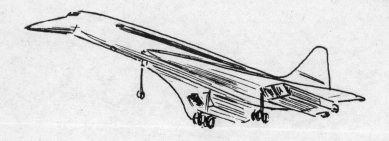

CAROUSEL BOOKS
A DIVISION OF TRANSWORLD PUBLISHERS LTD.

CONTENTS

MAKING THE MODELS

Detailed instructions are given for each model but there are several instructions which cover all of them, and these should be read through carefully before you begin.

If you follow the instructions precisely, stage by stage, you should have no difficulty in completing the models. Remember that the care you put into their building will be reflected in the finished aircraft. Take your time, be sure you understand how the parts are assembled before you glue them into place. If you rush the work, and take short cuts, the models will not be as good as they would have been had you taken more time and worked carefully.

BEFORE YOU START YOU WILL NEED

TOOLS

Pencil
Ruler
Compass
Scissors
Sharp craft knife
Carbon paper
Glass paper
Pins

MATERIALS

Thin card
Stiff card
2.5mm balsa sheet
Balsa block
Tracing paper
1.00mm plywood
Square balsa strip
Cardboard tubes
Cocktail sticks
Glue (white PVA is ideal)
Adhesive tape
Paint — Emulsion and polymer paints are ideal
Varnish — a medium gloss is best

Check before you begin a particular model that you have all the materials for the parts required and necessary tools to hand. Not all the above materials are necessary for each model.

GENERAL INSTRUCTIONS

You will need to transfer the plans for each piece of the model to the balsa sheet or card you are using.

1. Place a piece of carbon paper and the card or *balsa sheet under the part to be made.

    Draw carefully round the shape with a sharp pencil.

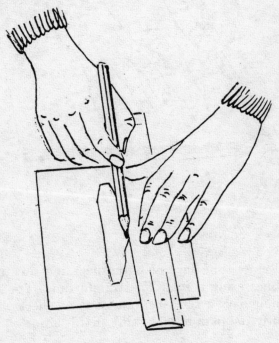

*When marking out the balsa parts, the grain of the wood may distort the shape, so check your marking out with a ruler before starting to cut the pieces.

2. Use your compass to prick the corners and any other details. You will find many dotted lines showing the correct positions for fitting the parts together.

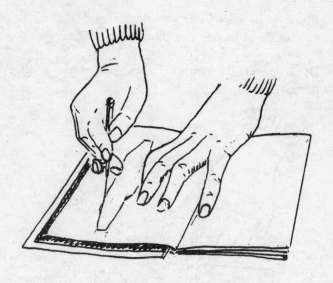

3. Remove the card or balsa sheet and tidy up your lines using a ruler for straight lines. You should now have a very accurate copy — check with the original plan to make sure that it is one!

4. Cut out the plan and score any broken lines signifying a tab or fold with a ruler and the point of your compass.

Arrows shown on parts always point to the front of the model, and most of the models have a general arrangement drawing or side view to help you identify and locate the various pieces.

During the construction you can trim the edges of your model, both the card and balsa, with a sharp craft knife and finish off with glass paper.

The finished model can be painted any colour you choose, the military ones should, of course, be in camouflage, and transfers and markings should be applied before the final varnishing.

PIPER WARRIOR

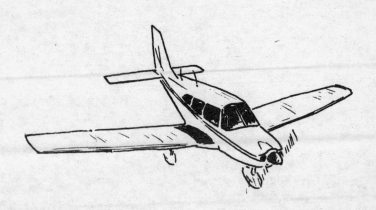

PIPER WARRIOR

The Piper Aircraft Corporation are one of the leading producers of light aeroplanes which are in regular service throughout the world. There are models ranging from a single seat agricultural aircraft up to the ten-seater commuter plane.

The Warrior first flew in 1972 and is very popular with flying clubs and private owners. It is a four-seat low-wing monoplace with a maximum speed of about 150 mph (240 km/h) which can be fully equipped with an auto-pilot and sophisticated navigational equipment to make it a very safe and reliable machine.

Manufacturer: Piper Aircraft Corporation U.S.A.

Power Plant: One Lycoming flat-four engine

Wing span: 10.67m

Overall length: 7.25m

PIPER WARRIOR

Building instructions

Parts required:

a) 2.5mm balsa sheet

Base
Spine
Fuselage top
Bulkhead (2 parts)
Nose

b) Card

Fuselage side (2 required)
Windscreen
Wing base
Wing top (2 required)
Tail-plane
Rudder
Propellor

c) Cocktail sticks for undercarriage
3 Wheel covers — 5mm balsa block
3 wheels — 4mm diameter semi-circles, 2.5mm balsa
Wing strengtheners — 2.5 × 5mm balsa (2 required)
Propellor circle — clear plastic

Construction:

1. Cut out the base, spine and fuselage top, following the general instructions on page 9. The base should be partially cut through, along the broken line a—b on the plan, to form a V. This will allow it to be bent to follow the line of the spine.

   Glue the spine along the base as indicated by the dotted lines on the base plan, and centre and glue the fuselage top to the spine.

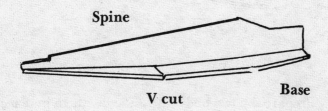

Spine

V cut   Base

2. Glue the two bulkhead pieces either side of the spine as shown with their bases positioned on the dotted lines c—d on the base plan.

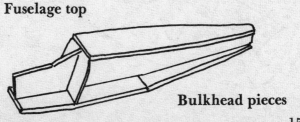

Fuselage top

Bulkhead pieces

3.   Fit the nose in place and sand the edges of the balsa wood structure to round them, paying particular attention to the top of the bulkhead where it joins the fuselage and the base of the nose, as shown on the plan page 20.

Rounded edges

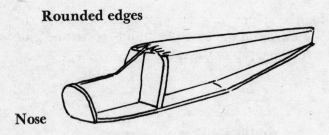

Nose

4.   Prepare the two body side and glue them in place, overlapping and glueing them to the spine at the front.

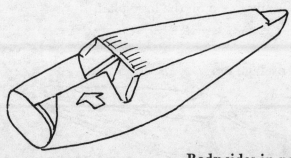

Body sides in position

5. Glue the main wing base to the bottom of the fuselage. Cut the wing strengtheners from balsa strip and taper them towards the tips. Glue these in place on the broken lines shown on the wing base plan.

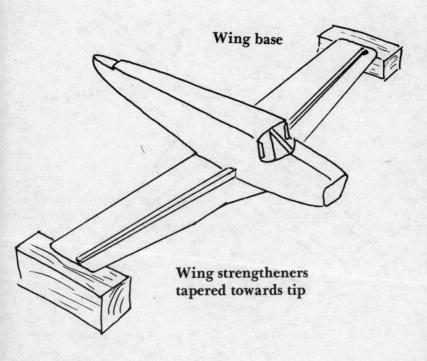

Wing base

Wing strengtheners tapered towards tip

Support the wing tips on blocks 10mm high and allow the glue to dry.

6. Prepare the two wing tops and fit them in place with the tabs glued to the underside of the wing base. Cut three 8mm pieces of cocktail stick and glue them into the holes marked on the fuselage base and wing base.

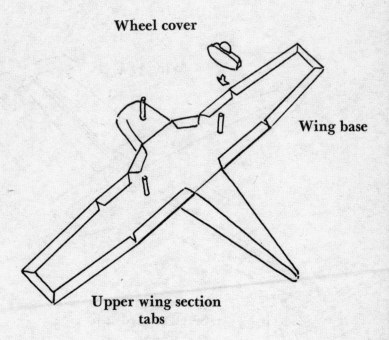

Wheel cover

Wing base

Upper wing section
tabs

Cut the wheel covers from 5mm thick balsa and sand them to the shape shown in the cross section, page 20. Glue on the semi-circles of balsa to form the wheels. Fix to the cocktail sticks.

7.   Run a fillet of glue along the joints where the wing tops meet the fuselage sides. Prepare the tail plane and rudder and fix them in place. Cut out the windscreen section and glue this in place.

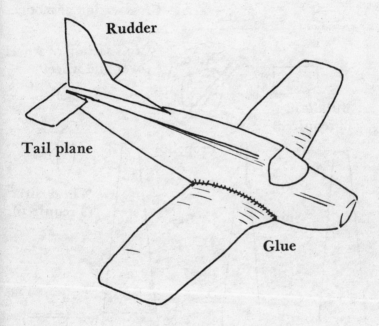

Rudder

Tail plane

Glue

Cut the propeller and fit in place with a pin. If the model is to be displayed in flight, a circle of clear plastic should be fitted in place of the propeller as this would not be visible during flight.

The model may now be painted and varnished in the colour and markings of your choice.

PLANS

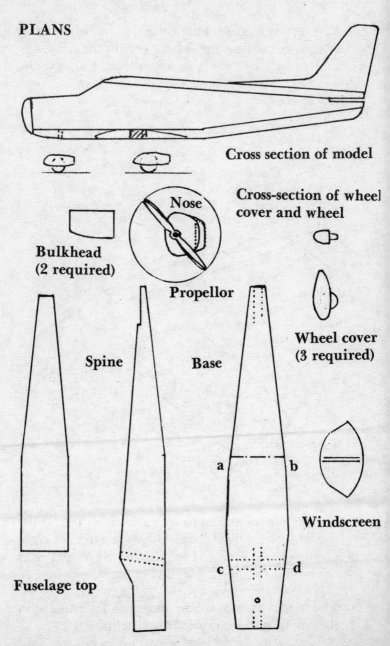

Cross section of model

Cross-section of wheel cover and wheel

Bulkhead (2 required)

Nose

Propellor

Wheel cover (3 required)

Spine

Base

Windscreen

a   b

c   d

Fuselage top

20

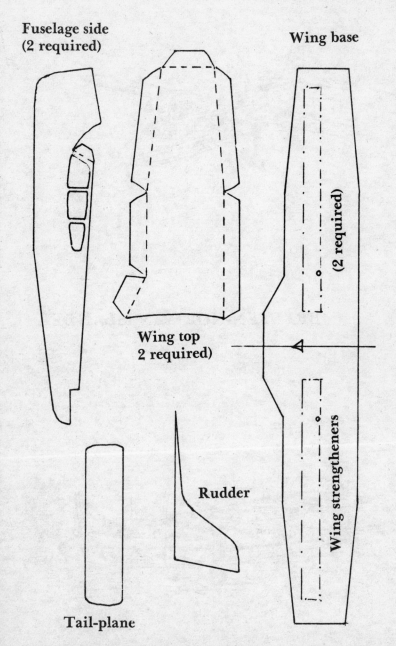

Fuselage side
(2 required)

Wing base

Wing top
2 required)

(2 required)

Wing strengtheners

Rudder

Tail-plane

BRITTEN-NORMAN ISLANDER

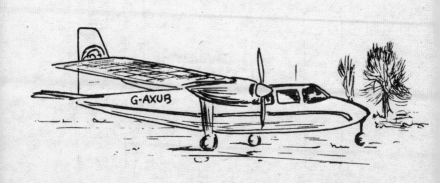

BRITTEN-NORMAN ISLANDER

This Islander is a ten-seat, twin-engined aircraft designed for light commercial duties and particularly for service between small islands without real airport facilities. The first prototype flew in 1965 and the first production aircraft were delivered in 1967.

Several versions have been developed, including an enlarged model with three engines called the Trislander, a military version called the Defender adapted for a wide variety of roles such as search and rescue, security, patrol, transport and casualty duties. The Maritime Defender is equipped for coastal patrol, fishery and oil-rig protection and coastguard service.

Manufacturer: Britten-Norman Ltd. Isle of Wight

Power plant: Two Lycoming flat-six engines

Wing span: 14.94m or 16.15m

Overall length: 10.86m or 12.02m

BRITTEN-NORMAN ISLANDER

Building instructions

Parts required:

a) **2.5mm balsa sheet**

    Base
    Spine
    Fuselage top
    Nose (3 required)

b) **Card**

    Fuselage
    Windscreen
    Wing base
    Wing top
    Tail-plane
    Rudder
    Undercarriage cover (2 required)

c) Cocktail sticks for undercarriage legs
5 wheels − 5mm diameter × 2.5mm balsa
Wing strengtheners − 2.5 × 5mm balsa (2 required)
Stiff card for propellors or clear plastic for disc
Balsa block for engines (2 required)

Construction:

1. Transfer the plan of the wing base (only half of which is shown) onto a piece of card that has been folded, ensuring that line a—b runs along the fold of the card. Cut out the plan through the two layers of card and open out for the complete wing base.

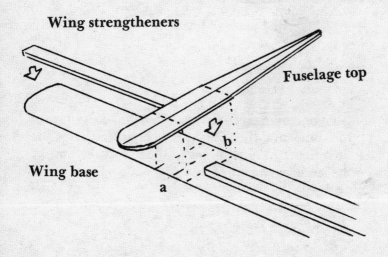

Centre and fix the wing base to the fuselage top between the dotted lines on the fuselage top plan. Fix the two wing strengtheners along the broken lines on the wing base plan as shown.

2. Glue the spine in place over the wing base.

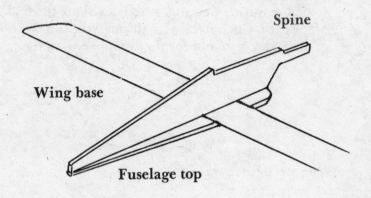

Spine

Wing base

Fuselage top

3. Glue one nose piece to the underside of the nose of the spine, and then fix the base beneath that. Glue the other two nose pieces to the top of the nose of the spine as shown.

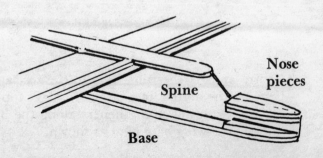

Nose pieces

Spine

Base

Put blocks under the wing tips to keep the structure square and leave to dry. When fully dry, shape the nose of the plane as shown on the cross-section, page 31. Also, sand and shape the fuselage top to a curve, and the back of the base to follow the line of the spine.

4. Prepare the main fuselage.

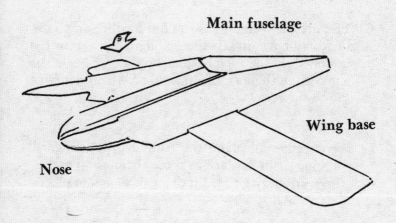

Main fuselage

Wing base

Nose

5. Glue the main fuselage in place. Begin with one side, then fold across the tapered base section, and finally the second side.

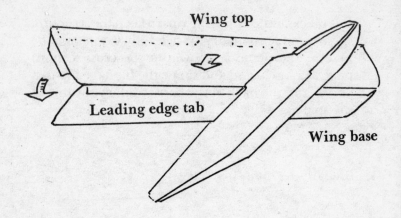

Wing top

Leading edge tab

Wing base

6. Prepare the wing top as you did for the wing base, instruction 1. Attach the leading edge tab to the underside of the wing base as shown, shape over the wing strengtheners and then fix the trailing edge tab to the rear.

7. Prepare the tail-plane and rudder from stiff card and glue them in place as shown below and on the cross section, page 31. Fit the windscreen in place.

Windscreen

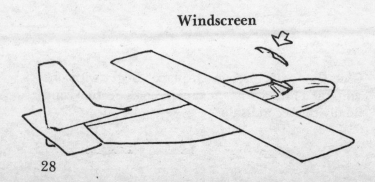

8. To prepare the undercarriage legs, take a length of cocktail stick 20mm long and wrap and glue the undercarriage cover around it. Attach two wheels either side of the leg as shown.

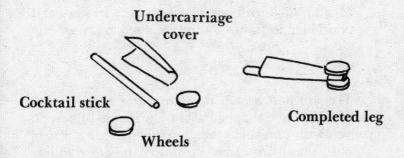

Undercarriage cover

Cocktail stick

Wheels

Completed leg

9. The engines are made from balsa block 10mm × 10mm and 25mm long, cut and sanded to shape as shown on the plans and cross-sections page 33.

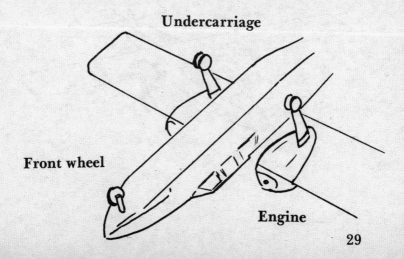

Undercarriage

Front wheel

Engine

Attach the undercarriage legs in the holes shown on the engine plan so that the undercarriage cover fits flush to the engine. Glue them to the wings in the positions shown on the wing base plan.

The front wheel is prepared from a 6mm length of cocktail stick with one wheel glued to its side, and positioned as shown on the cross-section, page 31.

10. Prepare and attach the propellors, with a small piece of balsa shaped to form the propellor nose. If you wish to display the plane flying, cut a disc of clear plastic instead of the propellor before adding the propellor nose.

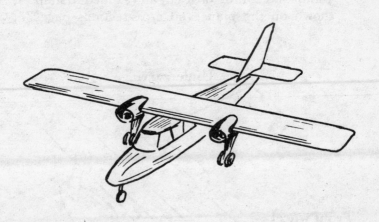

PLANS

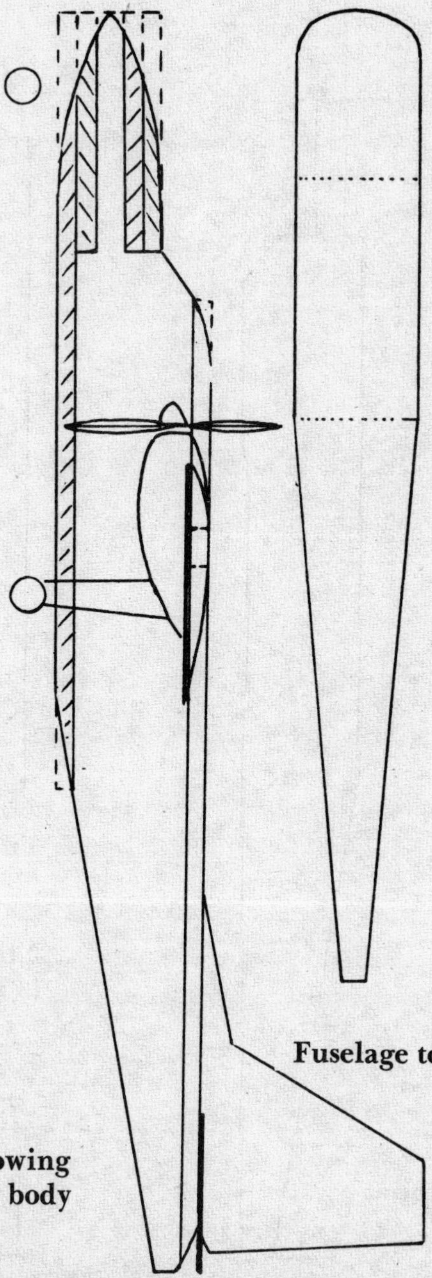

Fuselage top

Cross-section showing
shaping of main body
structure

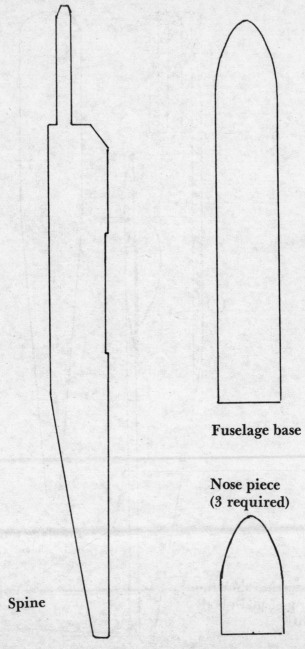

Fuselage base

Nose piece
(3 required)

Spine

32

Engine and propellor nose

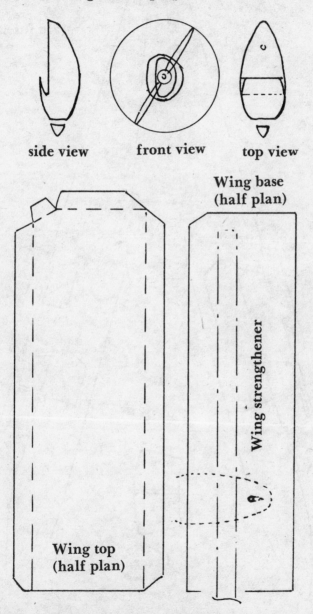

side view

front view

top view

Wing base
(half plan)

Wing strengthener

Wing top
(half plan)

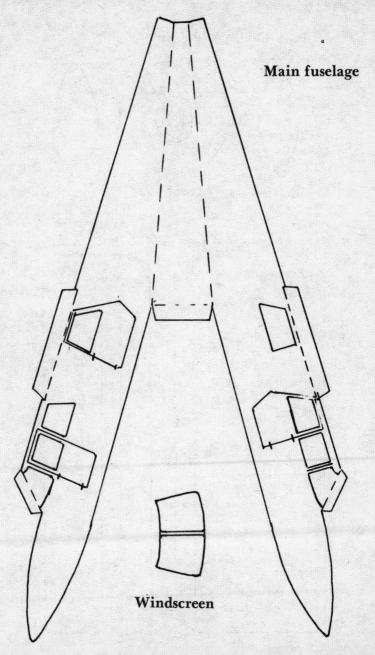

Main fuselage

Windscreen

Tail-plane

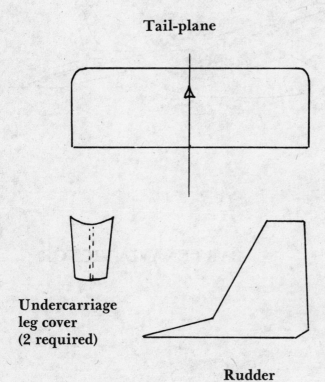

**Undercarriage
leg cover
(2 required)**

Rudder

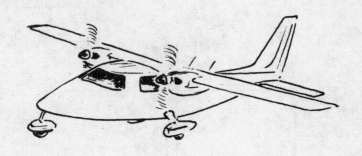

PARTENAVIA VICTOR

PARTENAVIA P. 68B VICTOR

The Partenavia company was formed in 1957 to produce light aircraft. In 1974 the company moved to a factory at Naples Airport and concentrated on production on a two/four seat basic training aircraft and the various models of the P68 Victor. The P. 68B Victor is a twin-engined seven seat business/commercial aircraft and has been in production since 1974. There is also an amphibious version fitted with floats. The P. 68 Observer is a version modified in Germany for Police and Coastguard duties, the Plexiglas nose gives a forward and downward view equal to that of a helicopter.

Manufacturer: Partenavia. Italy

Power plant: Two 200 hp Lycoming flat-four engines

Wing span: 12.00m

Overall length: 9.35m

PARTENAVIA VICTOR

Building instructions

Parts required:

a) **2.5mm balsa sheet**

   Base
   Spine
   Fuselage top
   Bulkhead (2 parts)

b) **Card**

   Fuselage side (2 required)
   Wing base
   Wing top
   Tail-plane
   Rudder

c) Wing strengthener − 2.5 × 5mm balsa
   Cocktail sticks for undercarriage
   Stiff card for propellors
   3 wheels − 5mm diameter
   10mm × 10mm balsa block for engines

Construction:

1. Assemble the balsa body parts. The base should be
    partially cut through in a 'v' shape, from a−b and
    c−d on the base plan, to allow it to bend to fit the
    shape of the spine. The two bulkheads fitted just
    behind the nose crease of the base.

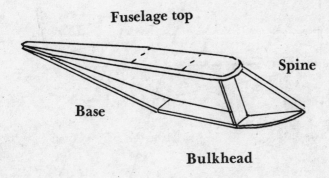

2. Glue the body sides in place, joining them at the
    nose along the front edge of the spine.

    Fix the wing strengthener to the wing base, and
    then fold round the wing top, beginning with the
    leading edge tab. Centre the completed wing over
    the fuselage top, fixing it in place between the
    dotted lines shown on the plan.

Cut a notch 18mm deep in the tail of the plane between the base and fuselage top. Insert the tail plane. Fix the rudder along the fuselage top to the point indicated on the tail plane.

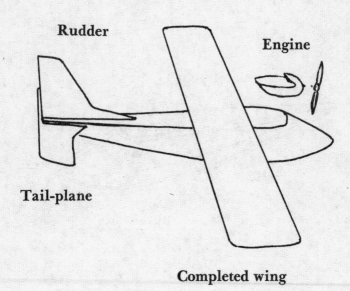

Rudder

Engine

Tail-plane

Completed wing

Shape two engines from the 10mm × 10mm piece of balsa block, each 22mm long, as shown on the plan and views, page 45. Cut the propellors from thick card and glue in place, finishing with the propellor nose piece cut and shaped from balsa. Fix the engines in place at the positions shown by the dotted lines on the wing plan.

3. Cut two 12mm lengths and one 10mm length of cocktail stick for the undercarriage struts. Glue in the holes provided on the base plan at the angle shown below. Fix the wheels as shown and allow to dry before supporting the plane on them.

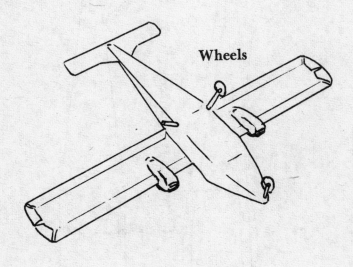

Wheels

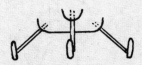

PLANS

Base

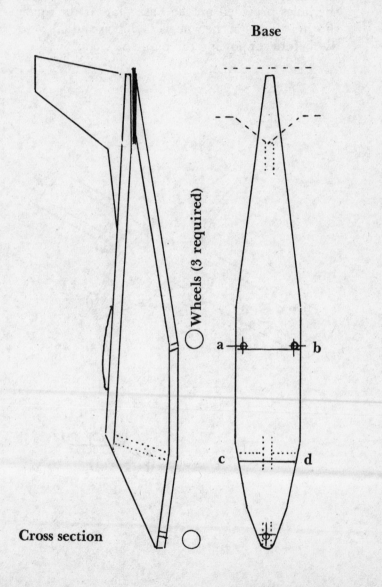

Wheels (3 required)

a   b

c   d

Cross section

42

Fuselage top

**Fuselage side
(2 required)**

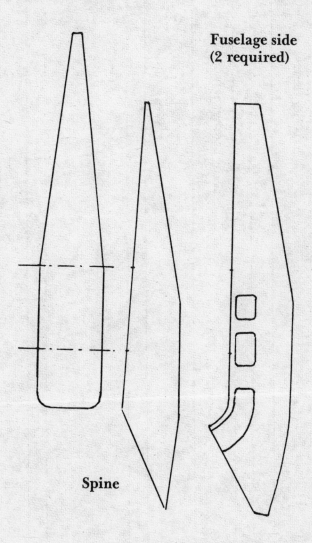

Spine

43

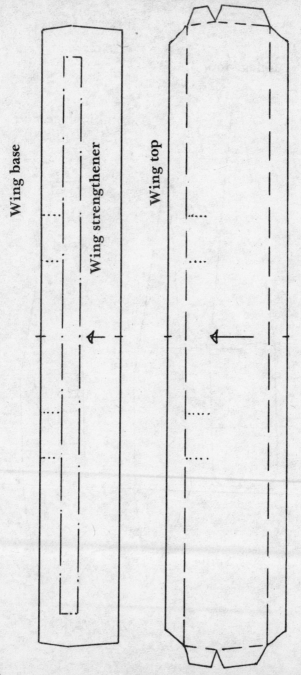

Wing base

Wing strengthener

Wing top

44

Engine and propellor

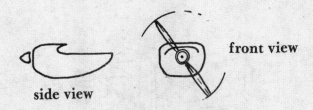

side view

front view

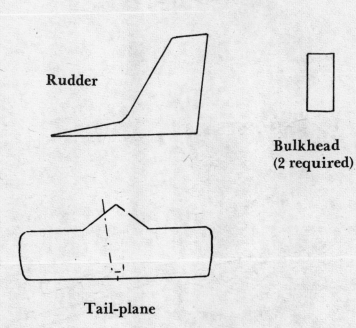

Rudder

Bulkhead
(2 required)

Tail-plane

SHORTS 330

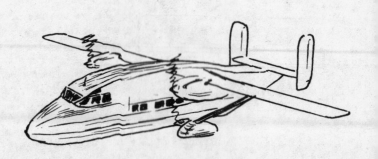

SHORTS 330

Short Brothers opened the first British aircraft factory in 1909 to build Wright Flyers and have been a major aeronautical company ever since, currently producing light transports for use all over the world for passenger, freight, survey, military and general commercial duties.

The 330 is a 30 seat twin-engined aircraft designed for commuter and local air service operations. The first prototype flew in 1974 and initial deliveries began in 1976. A Military version, capable of transporting troops and vehicles, supply dropping and general support duties is also produced.

Manufacturer: Short Brothers Ltd. Northern Ireland

Power plant: Two Pratt and Whitney turboprop engines

Wing span: 22.76m

Overall length: 17.69

SHORTS 330

Building instructions

Parts required:

a) **2.5mm balsa sheet**

   Base (3 parts)
   Spine (2 parts)
   Centre bulkhead
   Front bulkhead (2 required)
   Undercarriage centre
   Wing struts (2 required)

b) **Card**

   Body front (2 required)
   Body rear (2 required)
   Body top − total length 255mm
   Wing top (2 required)

c) **Stiff card or thin plywood**

   Wing base (2 required)
   Rear wing
   Rudder (2 required)
   2 Propellors

d) Balsa block for engines and wheel covers
   2 wheels − 10mm diameter semi-circles from 4 mm thick balsa

2 wheels — 5mm diameter balsa sheet circles
Clear plastic for propellor discs if required
Wing strengthener — 2.5 × 5mm
Cocktail stick for front undercarriage

Construction:

1. Glue the centre bulkhead to the dotted lines **c – d** on the main base. Attach the front and rear spine, and then the front and rear base parts.

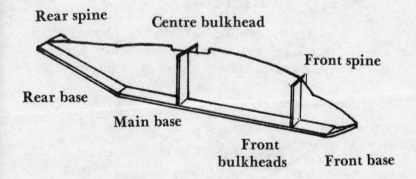

Rear spine

Centre bulkhead

Front spine

Rear base

Main base

Front bulkheads

Front base

Attach the front bulkheads either side of the front spine, positioning them on the dotted lines on the front spine plan and dotted line a – b on the main base plan.

2. Glue the body front and body rear sides in place, folding the top tabs inwards. Overlap the join at the centre of the bulkhead.

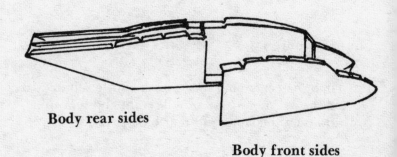

Body rear sides

Body front sides

3. Prepare the two halves of the wing base and join them together at the centre. Glue the wing strengthener in place on the broken line markings.

Wing in place

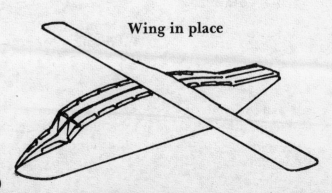

Fix the two halves of the wing top in place, beginning with the leading edge as usual. The completed wing is then fitted into the slot in the fuselage top.

4. Cut two strips of card 30mm wide × 65mm long for the front and 30mm × 55mm for the rear. Weave these under and over the tabs of the body sides as shown to strengthen and hold the body in shape.

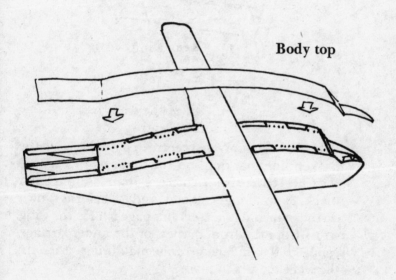

Body top

The plan of the body top has to be extended to a total length of 255mm as indicated. Glue in place starting with the nose and windscreen.

5. The rear wing and the two rudders should be cut from stiff card or thin plywood and assembled before fitting the model. Use pins to hold the pieces together while the glue dries and strengthen the corners with small strips of balsa as shown in the diagram.

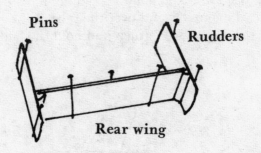

Pins

Rudders

Rear wing

6. Glue the undercarriage centre in place between the broken line markings on the main base. Prepare the wheel covers from a piece of 8mm × 8mm balsa block, 35mm long. Cut and sand to shape as shown on the plan and cross-section, page 59. Fix the wing struts from the front corners of the undercarriage centre to the underside of the main wings, then fix the wheel covers in place.

Prepare the engines from 15mm × 15mm balsa block, 47mm long, shaping them as shown on the plans, page 59. Pin the propellor in place.

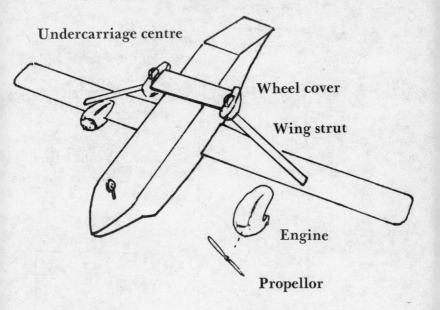

Undercarriage centre

Wheel cover

Wing strut

Engine

Propellor

Cut a piece of cocktail stick 8 long and glue in the hole marked on the main base. Glue the two 5mm diameter wheels in place. Glue the 10mm semi-circles to the base of the wheel covers.

7. Centre and glue the rear wing assembly to the top of the rear of the body. Paint the model the colour of your choice, remembering to paint the windows.

PLANS

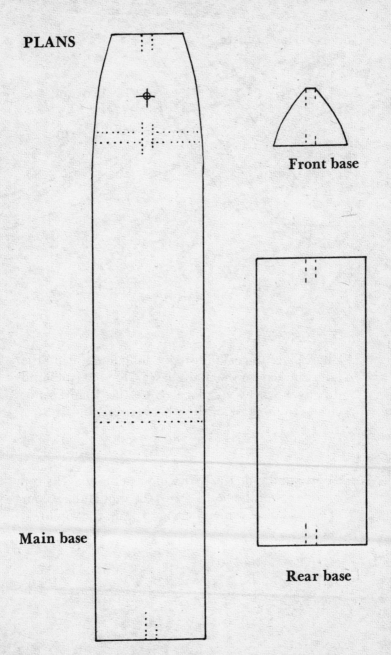

Front base

Main base

Rear base

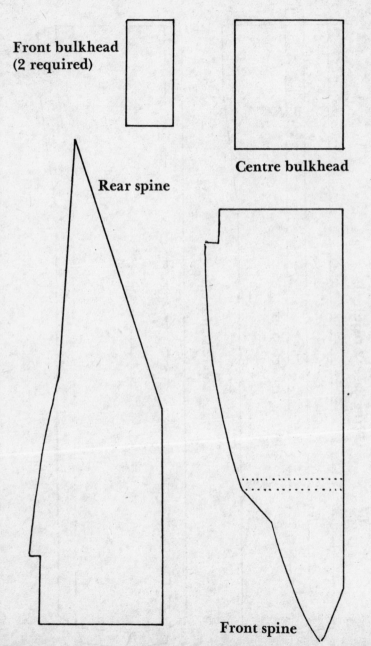

Front bulkhead (2 required)

Centre bulkhead

Rear spine

Front spine

55

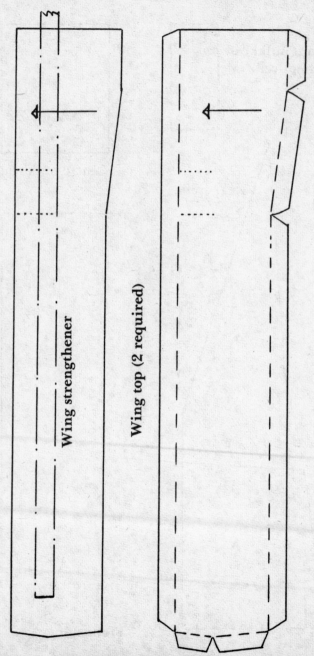

Wing base (2 required)

Wing strengthener

Wing top (2 required)

Body rear
(2 required)

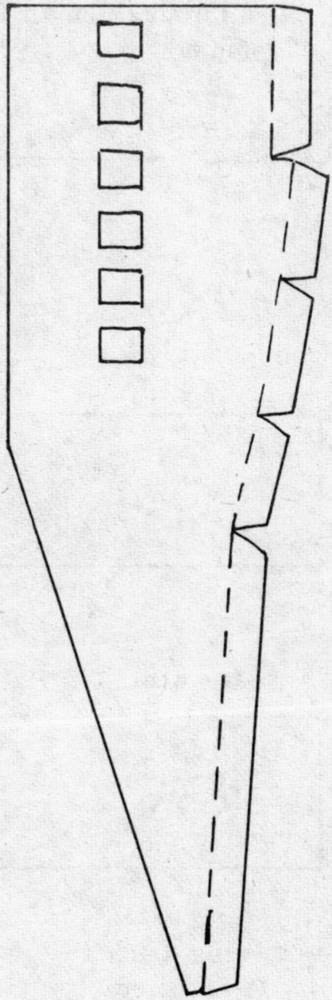

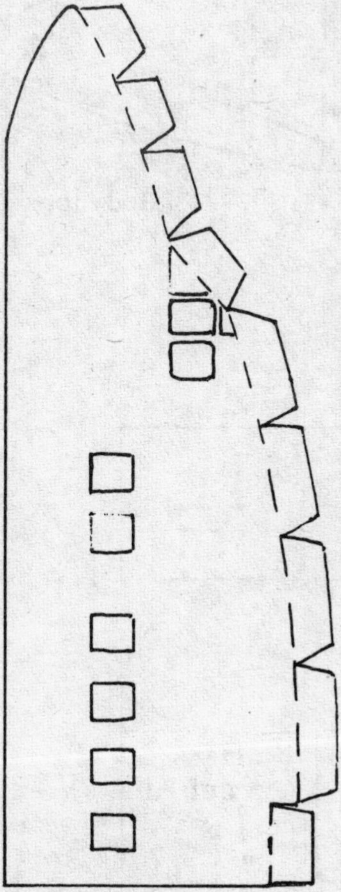

Body front
(2 required)

57

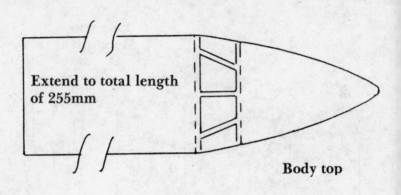

Extend to total length
of 255mm

Body top

Rear wing

**Rudder
(2 required)**

**Wing struts
(2 required)**

58

Wheel cover (2 required)

top view

front view

Engine (2 required)

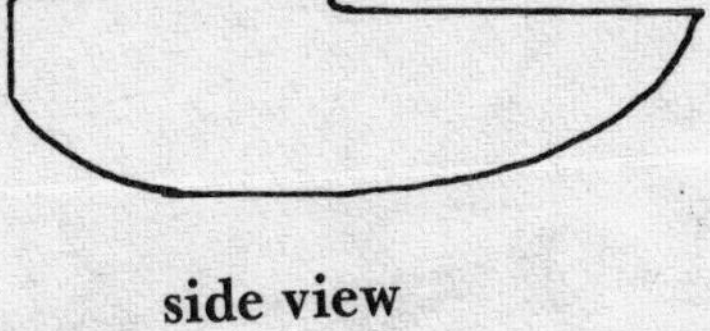

Propellor

side view

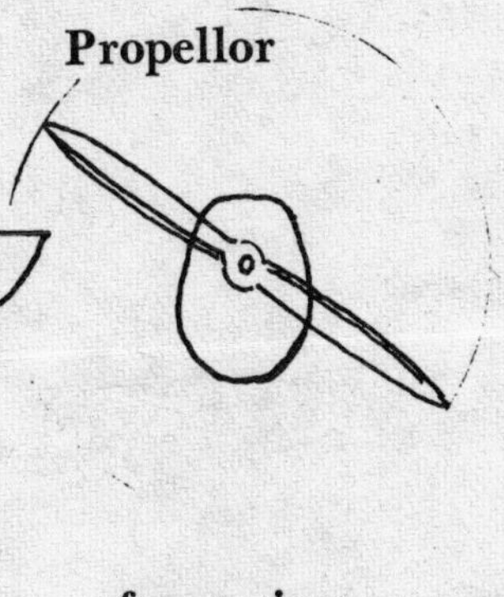

front view

SEPECAT JAGUAR

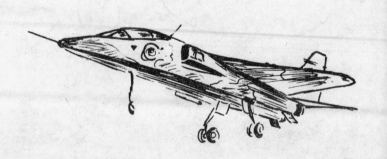

SEPECAT JAGUAR

Sepecat is an Anglo-French company formed in 1966 by the British Aircraft Corporation and Breguet Aviation to design and produce a supersonic strike fighter/Trainer. The first prototype Jaguar flew in 1969 and production models entered service in 1973. Several different versions have been made to fulfil specific duties with the French Air Force and the R.A.F. As a single-seat tactical support aircraft the Jaguar has proved to be very successful with very good performance, light-weight and computer controls. Maximum level speed is better than Mach 1.5, equivalent to 990 mph (1593 km/h).

Manufacturer: British Aerospace and Avions Marcel Dassault/Breguet Aviation

Power Plant: Two Rolls-Royce/Turbomeca Adour. Mk 102 turbofan engines

Wing Span: 8.69m

Overall length: 16.83m or 17.53m

SEPECAT JAGUAR

Building instructions

Parts required:

a)   2.5mm balsa sheet

   Base (2 parts)
   Rear spine
   Cockpit base

b)   Card

   Main fuselage
   Rear fuselage
   Main wing
   Rear wing (2 required)
   Rudder
   Cockpit cover
   Engine intakes (2 required)

c)   Pen tops or dowel 12mm diameter (2 required)
   Cocktail sticks for undercarriage if required
   Wheels − 2.5mm balsa sheet

Construction:

1. Assemble the main and front base parts, and the rear spine.

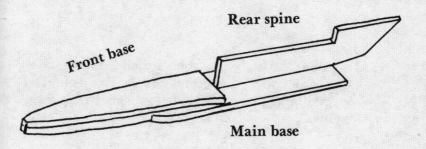

Rear spine

Front base

Main base

2. Fix the two pen tops or dowel either side of the spine as shown on the base plan, page 68. Tape in place with adhesive tape or a strip of thin card.

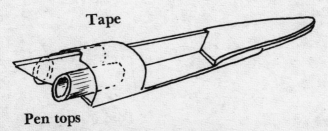

Tape

Pen tops

Main fuselage

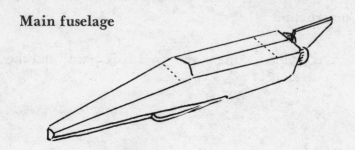

3.   Cut out the main fuselage. Attach it on one side, fold over and fix the second side, and then glue the overlapping pieces of the top to themselves and the spine.

4.   Prepare the main wings. The leading edges should be scored along lines a−b and c−d and the extra card folded under and glued against the wings to strengthen them. Trim any overlap to shape.

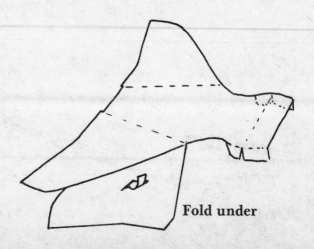

Fold under

5. Glue the wings in place on the main fuselage, fixing the centre back to the dotted line on the fuselage.

Wing section in position

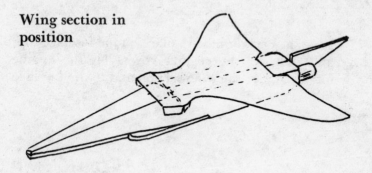

6. Prepare the rear fuselage. Glue in place along the top of the spine and over the rear of the wing. Then curve the two sides down and glue them to the base. Trim off any excess when glue is dry.

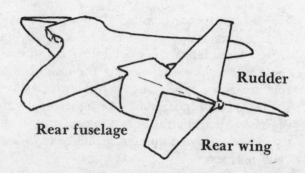

Rudder

Rear fuselage

Rear wing

Glue the rudder in place and the rear wings. The rear wings should be fitted just below the top edge of the body rear and slope down to the level of the body main base.

7. Glue the cockpit base in place on the fuselage top, and then fit the cockpit cover. Fit the engine intakes under the wing section and to the fuselage side.

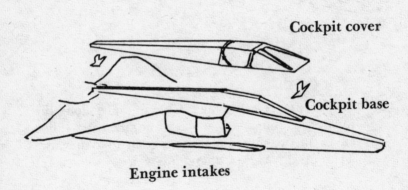

Cockpit cover

Cockpit base

Engine intakes

8. If you wish to display the model with the undercarriage down, this can be made by cutting three 15mm lengths of cocktail stick and inserting these in the holes marked on the main base. The rear struts should be angled forwards as shown on the cross-section, page 67. A single wheel, 6mm in diameter should be attached to the front strut, and two wheels, 8mm diameter, attached to the sides of each rear struts.

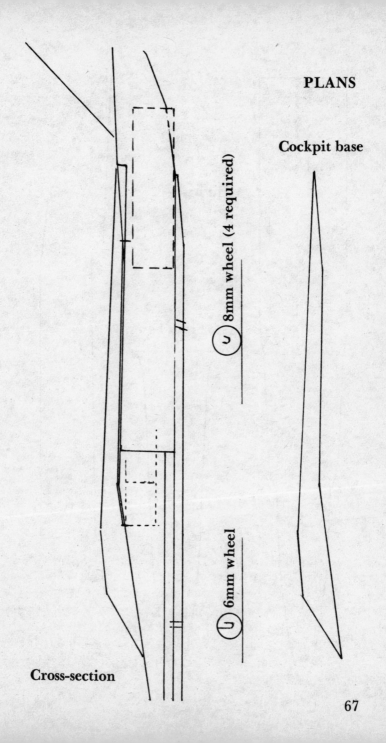

PLANS

Cockpit base

8mm wheel (4 required)

C 8mm wheel (4 required)

C 6mm wheel

Cross-section

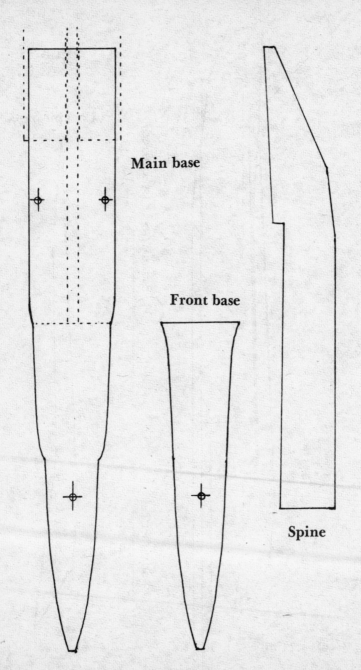

Main base

Front base

Spine

68

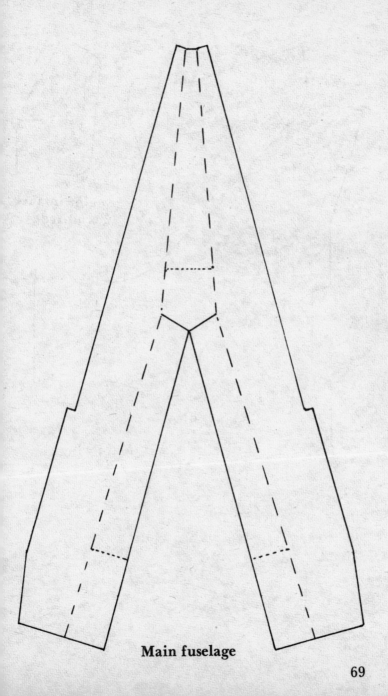

Main fuselage

69

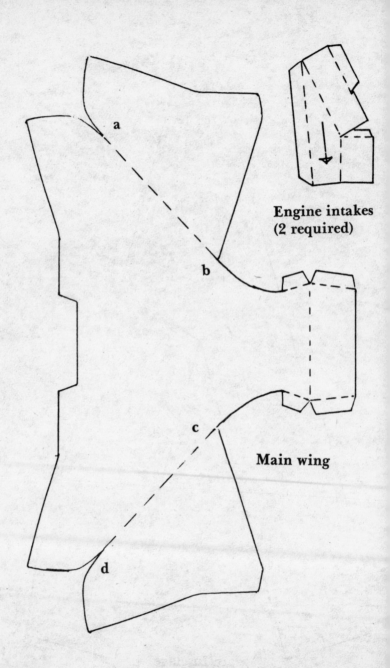

**Engine intakes
(2 required)**

Main wing

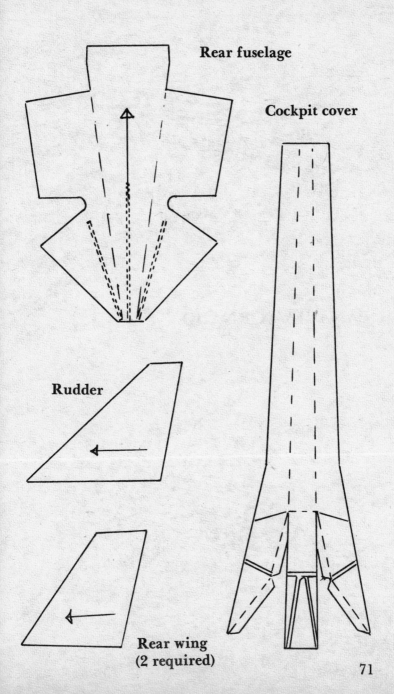

Rear fuselage

Cockpit cover

Rudder

Rear wing
(2 required)

71

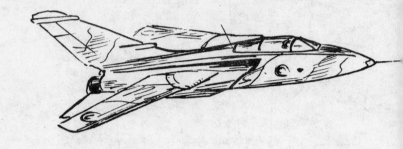

PANAVIA TORNADO

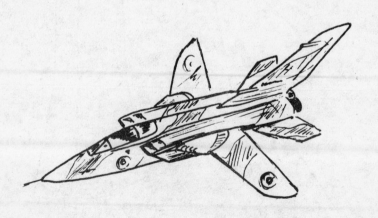

PANAVIA TORNADO

Panavia Aircraft Gmbh was formed in 1969 by British Aerospace, Messerschmitt and Aeritalia to develop a multi-role combat aircraft (MRCA) to be used by the airforces of Great Britain, Germany and Italy. The first prototype flew in August 1974 and production models are now in full service fulfilling duties previously performed by several different aircraft.

The Tornado is a 'swing wing' aircraft, the wings, when fully spread, allow relatively low speed manouvering and, when fully swept, give the aircraft a top speed in excess of Mach 1.93, equivalent to 1275 mph (2053 km/h).

Manufacturer: Panavia Aircraft

Power Plant: Two Turbo-Union RB. 199—34 R — 04 turbo-fan engines

Wing span: Spread 13.90m Swept 8.60m

Overall length: 16.70m

PANAVIA TORNADO

Building instructions

Parts required:

a)   2.5mm balsa sheet

>   Lower base (2 parts)
>   Upper base
>   Spine (3 parts)
>   Body side (2 required)
>   Nose side (2 required)
>   Nose top

b)   Stiff card or 1.0mm ply-wood

>   Fuselage lower top
>   Fuselage upper top
>   Main wing (2 required)

c)   Card

>   Fuselage top
>   Cockpit
>   Tail-plane (2 required)
>   Rudder
>   Engine intake (2 required)

d)   Cocktail sticks
Scrap sheet balsa
2 pen tops or 10mm dowel for engines

Construction:

1. Partially cut through a v-shape in the main lower base section at line a−b. Shave the inside edges where the nose and main sections of the lower base meet. Sand down the shaded areas of the upper base section.

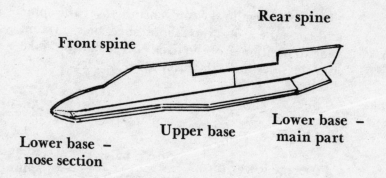

Rear spine

Front spine

Lower base − main part

Upper base

Lower base − nose section

Assemble the spine and base sections so that upper base section is sandwiched between the spine and the base, its rear on the dotted line c−d on the lower base plan. The nose section of the lower base should be angled to meet the nose of the spine, and the rear tilted up to the rear spine.

2. Add the two nose sides, curving them to shape by partially cutting through on the dotted lines to make v shape grooves. Fit the two body sides as shown.

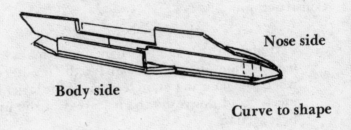

Nose side

Body side

Curve to shape

3. Fit the fuselage lower top centrally over the spine and cut a piece of scrap 2.5mm sheet balsa, 10mm wide to position over the back end as shown. Make sure the sides fit flush with the body sides.

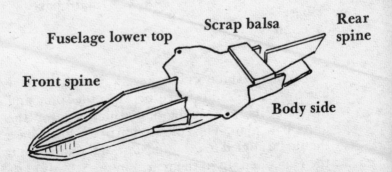

Fuselage lower top

Scrap balsa

Rear spine

Front spine

Body side

4. Glue the upper top in place over the scrap balsa strip and on to the two nose sides. Fit the central spine strip to complete the spine (shown dotted).

Fuselage upper top

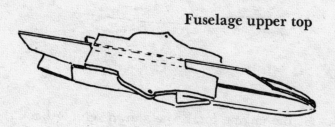

5. Prepare the two main wings and fit in palce with lengths of cocktail stick, remembering to glue the stick to the fuselage holes only to allow the wings to swing. Trim when dry.

Fit the nose top section. Sand to a smooth rounded shape when dry.

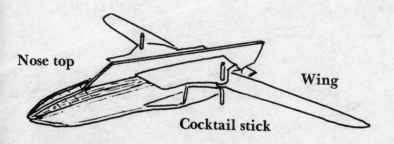

Nose top

Wing

Cocktail stick

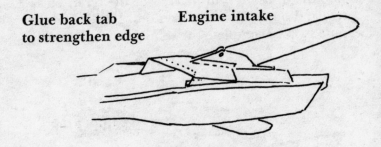

Glue back tab to strengthen edge　　**Engine intake**

6. Fit the engine intakes as shown, gluing back the leading edge tab to strengthen the front edge.

7. Fit the pen tops or dowel to form the engine jets so that they are level with the end of the spine. Glue the two outer sections of the fuselage top, leaving the centre free. Fix the glued areas either side of the base of the spine and around the body of the plane so that the spine becomes a curve.

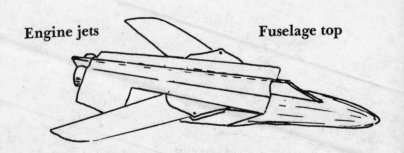

Engine jets　　**Fuselage top**

8. Glue the rudder in place, and the two tail-planes. Add the cockpit.

Cockpit

Rudder

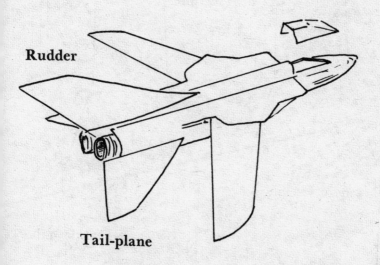

Tail-plane

9. An undercarriage may be added in the positions shown on the base plan, page 80. The front wheel is single, and the rear wheels double.

10. Finish the plane in camouflage.

PLANS

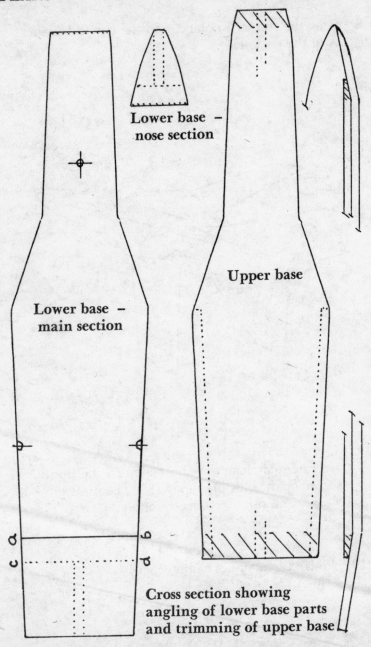

Lower base –
nose section

Upper base

Lower base –
main section

Cross section showing
angling of lower base parts
and trimming of upper base

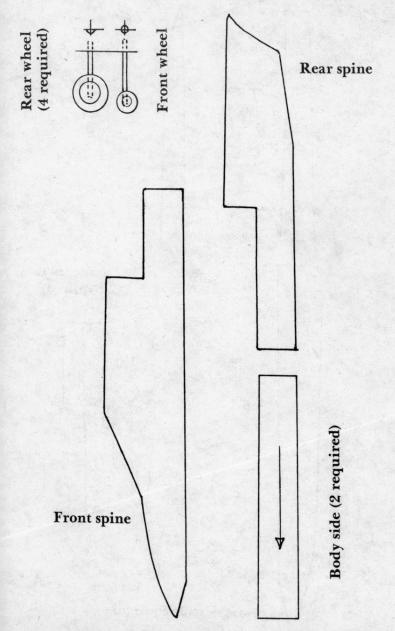

Rear wheel
(4 required)

Front wheel

Rear spine

Front spine

Body side (2 required)

81

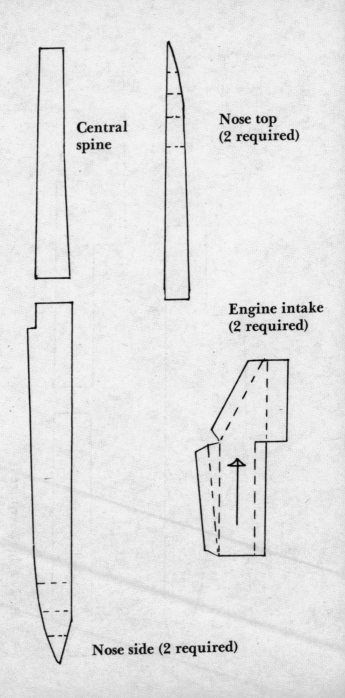

Central
spine

Nose top
(2 required)

Engine intake
(2 required)

Nose side (2 required)

82

Cockpit

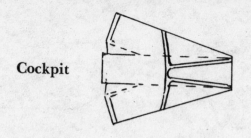

Fuselage top

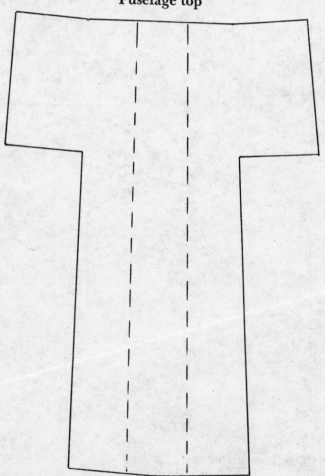

Fuselage upper top

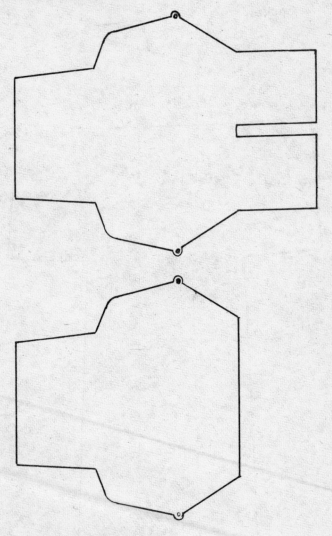

Fuselage lower top

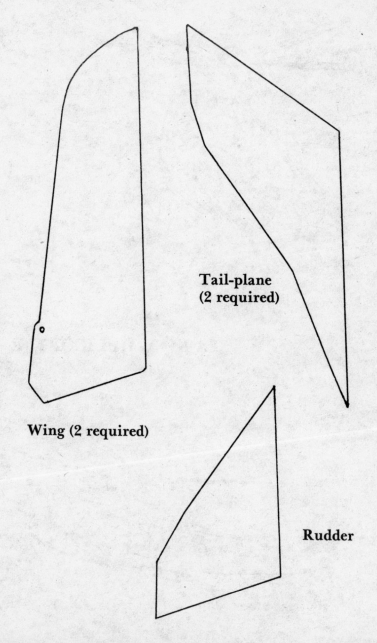

Tail-plane
(2 required)

Wing (2 required)

Rudder

85

SEA KING HELICOPTER

WESTLAND SEA KING

The Sea King was developed by Westland from the American sikorsky SH − 3D helicopter to provide the Royal Navy with an advanced anti-submarine and general purpose helicopter able to perform various support roles. The hull is designed to allow the Sea King to land on water in an emergency. Several versions have been developed and the HAR Mk3 is probably the finest search and rescue helicopter in service today.

The Sea King was used extensively in the recent Falklands Islands crisis in a wide variety of roles.

Manufacturer: Westland Aircraft Ltd. England

Power Plant: Two Rolls Royce Gnome turboshaft engines

Rotor diameter: 18.90m

Overall length: 22.15m

SEA KING HELICOPTER

Building instructions

Parts required:

a)   **2.5mm balsa sheet**

      Body base (2 required)
      Spine front
      Spine rear
      Centre bulkhead
      Front bulkhead (2 required)
      Body top (2 required)
      Rotor support (3 required)

b)   **Card**

      Body side (2 required)
      Body rear
      Rotor cowl base
      Rotor cowl top
      Windscreen
      Rear wing

c)   Undercarriage support — 2.5mm balsa 10mm
      wide × 42mm long
      Cocktail sticks
      Stiff card strips for main rotor
      Stiff card for tail rotor

4 wheels — 8mm diameter × 3mm thick
Rear wheel — 6mm diameter × 2.5mm thick
Balsa block for floats

Construction:

This model may appear to be very complicated but it should present no problems if you follow the instructions carefully, step by step.

1. Cut the two body bases partially through with a v-cut at line a−b to allow them to bend to fit the nose angle of the front spine. Glue them together with the front spine as shown, and fix the centre bulkhead in place.

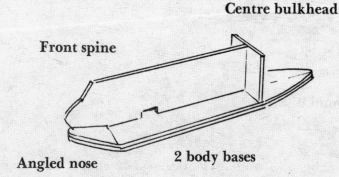

Centre bulkhead

Front spine

Angled nose

2 body bases

2. Fit the rear spine.

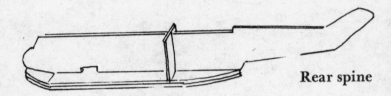

Rear spine

3. The two front bulkheads may now be positioned either side of the front spine, just behind the angle of the nose, and the two body tops glued together and fixed to the model.

Body tops

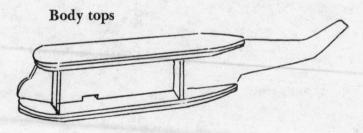

Front bulkhead

The nose and rear of the body should now be trimmed roughly to the shape shown on the cross-section, page 00 of the plans.

4. Sandwich and glue the three rotor support pieces together and fix in place in the position shown on the body top plan. If you wish to have your rotor free to turn, you will need to cut out the dotted section from the centre rotor support piece to allow it to take the rotor shaft. The rotor cowl base may now be fitted.

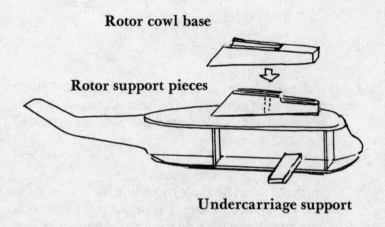

Rotor cowl base

Rotor support pieces

Undercarriage support

The undercarriage support cut from 2.5mm balsa, 10mm wide and 42mm long should be glued centrally through the gap provided in the spine.

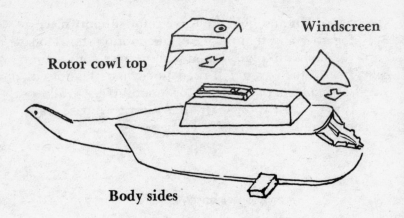

Rotor cowl top

Windscreen

Body sides

5. Fit the two body sides, followed by the windscreen and the rotor cowl top. The hole in the cowl top for the rotor shaft should be re-inforced with a circle of thin card if being used.

6. Finish the main fuselage by adding the rear section. Glue the centre of the card to the top of the rear spine and then each side is curved round and glued to the bottom edge and the body sides. Any excess card should be trimmed off when the glue is dry.

Body rear

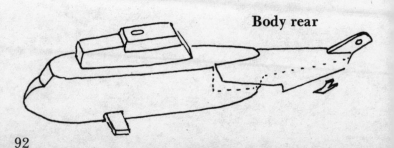

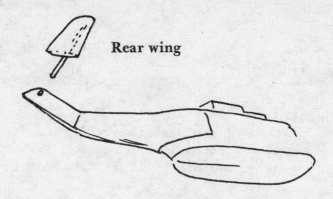

Rear wing

7. Make the rear wing around a piece of cocktail stick 30mm long, the end of which is passed through the hole marked in the rear spine and glued in place so that the rear wing fits flush to the body.

8. The rear rotor, cut from stiff card, is mounted on the end of the cocktail stick on the other side of the tail.

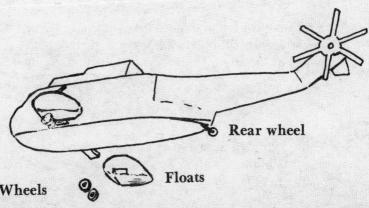

Rear wheel

Floats

Wheels

Shape the two floats from balsa block as shown on the plans and sections on page 101. Fit them on the ends of the undercarriage support with 28mm wheels beneath each.

Cut two 20mm lengths of cocktail stick for the float struts and position these from the top of the body sides to the inside edge of the top of the floats.

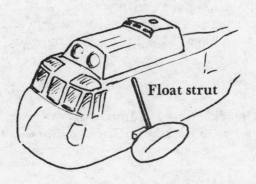

Float strut

The rear undercarriage strut is prepared from a 7mm length of cocktail stick and fitted with its wheel at an angle from the rear of the body base.

9.   The rotor blades are prepared as follows. Draw a circle 260mm in diameter and divide it into five segments (72° between each line).

Cut two small card discs, 15mm in diameter. Thread one disc over a cocktail stick from which the points have been cut. Stand the disc in the centre of the circle as shown below.

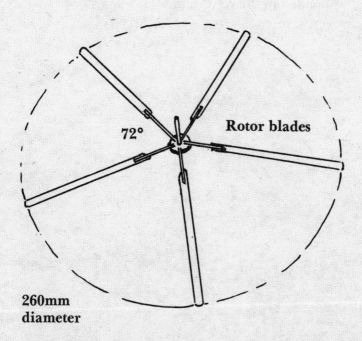

The rotor blades should be prepared and glued to 32mm lengths of cocktail stick as shown on the plans. Place the five blades on the lines of the five segments, remembering that their leading edges should point clockwise in the finished model – anti-clockwise as you lay them upside down on the circle. Glue the blades to the central disc.

Finally, thread and glue the second card disc over the central section to finish the blades. Leave to dry thoroughly.

When the glue is completely dry, trim the cocktail stick to a length to sit on the model through the hole provided in the cowl, and allow the rotor to turn.

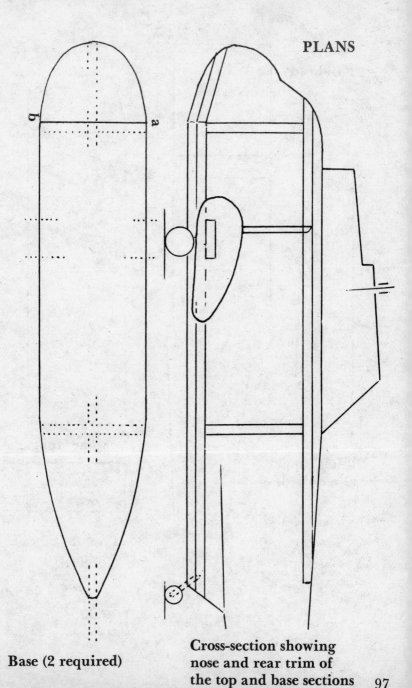

Base (2 required)

Cross-section showing nose and rear trim of the top and base sections

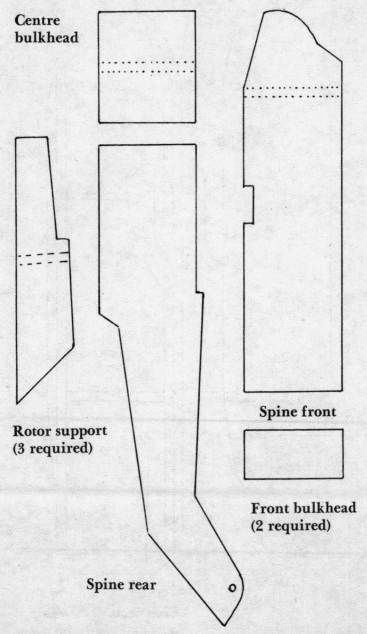

Centre bulkhead

Rotor support (3 required)

Spine front

Spine rear

Front bulkhead (2 required)

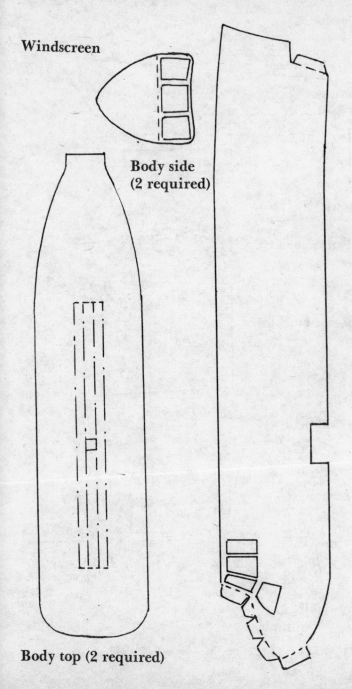

Windscreen

**Body side
(2 required)**

Body top (2 required)

99

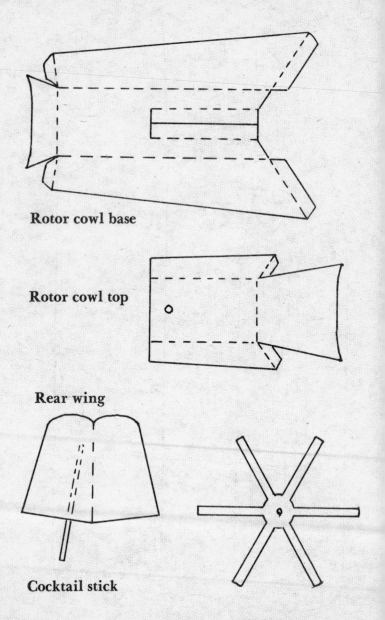

Rotor cowl base

Rotor cowl top

Rear wing

Cocktail stick

Tail rotor

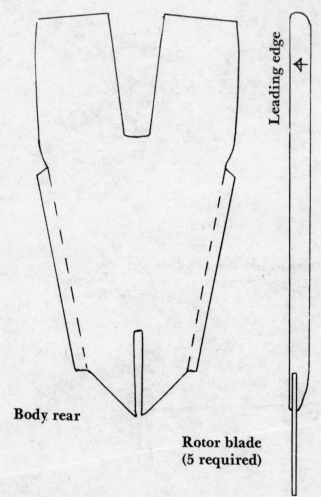

Body rear

**Rotor blade
(5 required)**

Leading edge

Float (2 required)

Cocktail stick

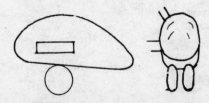

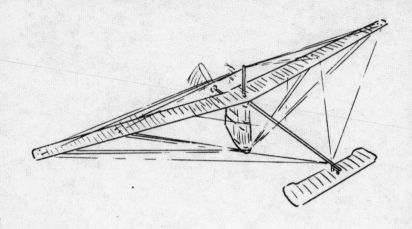

GOSSAMER ALBATROSS

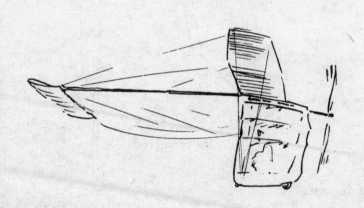

GOSSAMER ALBATROSS

For centuries man has wanted to fly, many have died while trying to achieve this 'impossible dream'. The first people took to the air in balloons and then flimsy bamboo and canvas kites and eventually petrol-engined machines. Man-powered flight seemed out of reach and large prizes were offered to the first over certain distances.

These major prizes have been won by an American, Paul MacCready, first with the Gossamer Condor and then with the Albatross which, in 1979, became the first man-powered machine to cross the English Channel. The Albatross is extremely light and carries just one person but the wingspan is 3 metres bigger than that of the Concorde.

Power plant: One very fit young man

Wing span: 28.6m

Overall length: 9.144m

GOSSAMER ALBATROSS

Building instructions

Parts required:

a)   **2.5mm balsa sheet**

Body top (2 required)
Body bottom (2 required)

b)   **Stiff card**

Body centre (2 required) — plan as for body bottom
Wing centre
Outer wing (2required)
Front wing

c)   **Thin paper** (tracing paper is ideal)

Main body
Wing covers

c)   Cocktail sticks or 1.5mm dowel
Thin thread
Propellor
Wing strengtheners — 1.5mm thick × 5mm wide balsa

Construction:

This is a delicate model, construction is quite straight-forward but great care is needed to achieve a good result.

1. Cut out the balsa and card body components, ensuring that the holes are the right size for the cocktail sticks or 1.5mm dowel.

   Assemble the main body as shown below, threading and gluing the body parts on a 65mm length of dowel at the positions and angles shown on the side view plan, page 109.

   A length of dowel 95mm long should be fixed into a hole made on the front of the body top sections at the angle shown on the side view plan and another length of dowel, 20mm long into a hole made at the rear as shown on the same plans.

   Allow the glue to dry thoroughly before sanding the base section to shape as shown below and the side view.

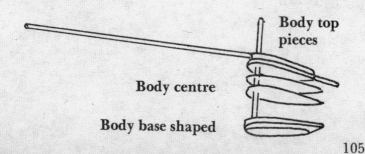

Body top pieces

Body centre

Body base shaped

2. Cut out and fit the main body cover.

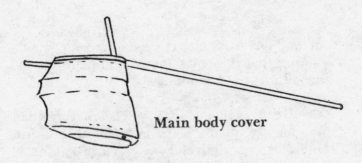

Main body cover

3. Join the three wing sections together, overlapping and gluing them on the shaded area. Fix the two wing strengtheners in place on the broken line area.

Pierce the central wing section hole large enough to take the cocktail stick or dowel of the body construction. Make small holes large enough to take a needle through the centres of the crosses marked on the wing sections, (a), (b), (c) and (d).

Cover the wings on both sides with tracing paper, joining the edges together under the wings.

Glue the wing in place.

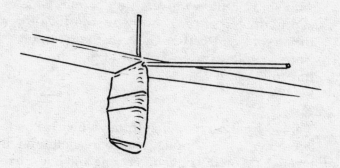

4. Prepare the front wing and mount it on the front boom as shown below and on the side-view plan, page 109, with a small square of 3mm × 3mm balsa for the spacer. Fix the propellor on the rear boots.

Make a small hole in the base of the body as marked on the side view plan, and cut a notch in the top of the centre post to allow you to fit the bracing wires.

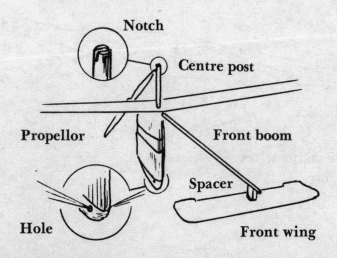

Thread a needle with very thin cotton. Glue one end to the top of the centre post and then thread the needle and cotton through the holes on the wings as follows, using a spot of glue to hold the thread in place.

Thread from centre notch through hole (a) on the left outer wing, through the base hole and up through (a) on the right outer wing and back to the centre.

Repeat from centre notch to hole (b) on the left outer wing, through the base and up through (b) on the right, then back to centre.

Continue in the same way through holes (c) and again through holes (d).

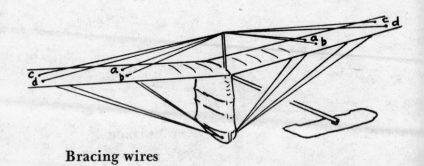

Bracing wires

PLANS

Side view plan showing assembly of body parts and shaping of body bottom

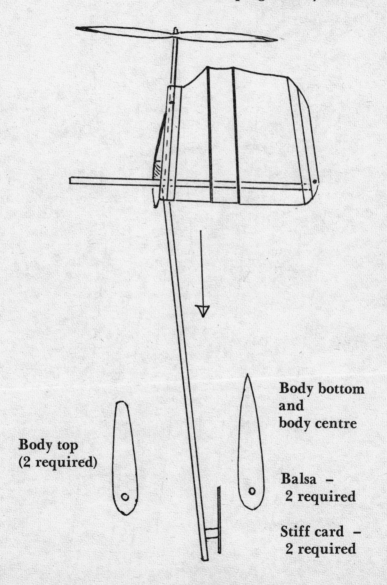

Body bottom
and
body centre

Body top
(2 required)

Balsa –
2 required

Stiff card –
2 required

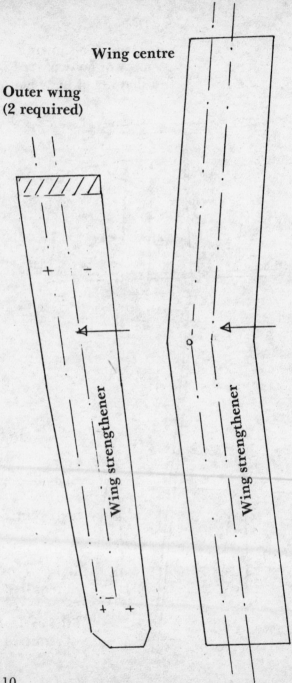

Wing centre

Outer wing
(2 required)

Wing strengthener

Wing strengthener

110

Main body

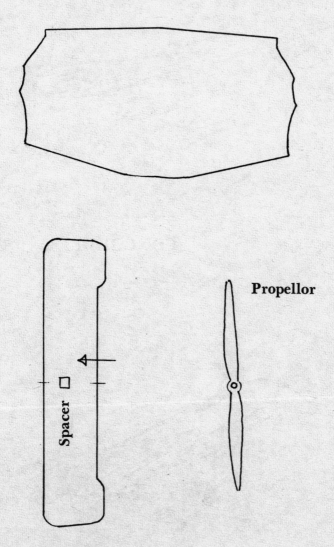

Propellor

Spacer

Front wing

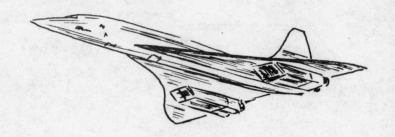

CONCORDE

CONCORDE

Concorde is probably the most talked about civil aircraft flying today. It was developed as a joint venture by the British and French governments, built in both countries and put into service by British Airways and Air France initially and later leased to several other airlines.

It is the fastest and most elegant aeroplane currently in service but economic and political pressures have prevented full development of the project. Concorde flies at supersonic speed, maximum cruising speed is Mach 2.04 — equivalent to 1354 mph (2179 km/h) — cutting the flying time from London or Paris to America by half.

Manufacturer:	British Aerospace and Aerospatiale
Power Plant:	Four Rolls-Royce/SNECMA Olympus 593 Mk 610 turbojet engines
Wing span:	25.56m
Overall length:	62.10m

CONCORDE

This model can be made in two sizes, the plans are to 1:144 scale but they are drawn on a 5mm square grid, which can be doubled to 10mm squares on your card to make the model to the same scale as the others in this book. The parts required list gives the alternative sizes. If you choose to make the larger model, you must carefully mark out a 10mm grid on your card, and then transfer the lines of the plans square by square.

Parts required:

1:144 scale (as plans)

20mm diameter × 325mm long cardboard tube
5mm square balsa strip
4 tubes — 8mm diameter × 4mm long
Wing base — card (half shown)
Wing base front — card (half shown)
Fuselage front — card 70mm long × 25mm wide
8 wheels — 8mm × 2mm
2 wheels — 6mm × 1.5mm

1:72 scale (using 10mm grid)

40mm diameter × 650mm long cardboard tube
10mm square balsa strip
4 tubes — 15mm diameter × 8mm long
Wing base — stiff card (half shown)
Wing base front — stiff card (half shown)
Fuselage front — card 140mm long × 45mm wide
8 wheels — 16mm × 5mm
2 wheels — 12mm × 3mm

For both scale models:

a) **Card**

> Wing top (2 required)
> Wing top front (2 required)
> Rudder
> Engine (2 required)
> Fuselage rear end

b) Cocktail sticks and card strip for undercarriage

Construction:

1. Prepare the fuselage tube by cutting across the mouth of the cardboard tube diagonally to a point 90mm (180mm for 1:72) from the end. Fold the two edges together leaving a 7mm diameter hole (14mm for 1:72) in the end and glue the offcut across the join to complete the tapered rear end.

Diagonal slice

Fuselage tube

Offcut used to secure the join

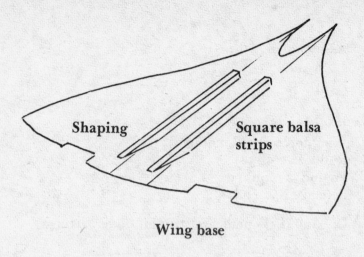

Shaping

Square balsa strips

Wing base

2. Double the plans of the wing base parts and cut from one piece of card. Glue or tape front to main section. Shape the shaded area on the ends of the square balsa strips. Glue in the position shown so that the trailing edge of the wing base tilts up.

3. Glue the fuselage tube to the wing base and balsa strips

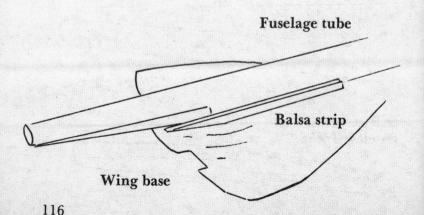

Fuselage tube

Balsa strip

Wing base

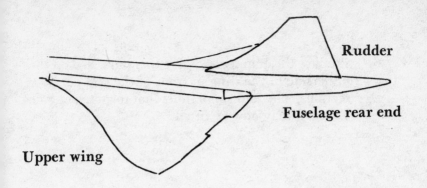

Rudder

Fuselage rear end

Upper wing

4. Roll the fuselage rear end into a cone. Glue to the rear of the fuselage. Prepare and fit the rudder from the point where the cone meets the fuselage.

   Cut out the wing top parts. Glue or tape the front and main wing sections together, and fit them to the plane, gluing the inside tabs over the balsa strips to the fuselage, and the outer edge tabs over the wing base.

5. Cut an oblong of card for the fuselage front 70mm long × 25mm wide (140mm long × 45mm wide for the 1:72 scale). Roll into a cone with a 5mm overlap at the open end and glue — the open end of the cone should now be 20mm wide (40mm for the 1:72 scale.)

   Make small cuts around the opening of the cone and glue it on to the fuselage.

Fuselage front

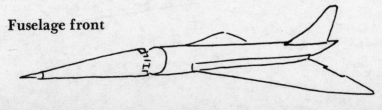

6. Prepare the engines and glue them in place on the underside of the wing in front of the two cutaway sections. The four small tubes that form the engine exhausts may now be fitted.

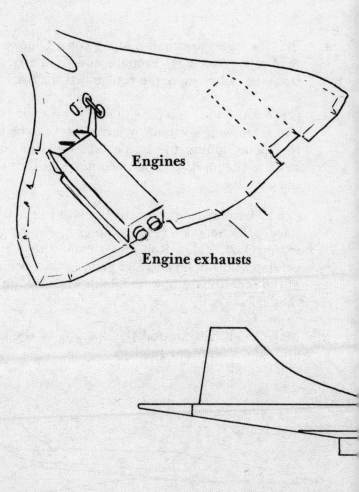

Engines

Engine exhausts

7. If you wish to display the model with its undercarriage down, cut two strips of scrap balsa 18mm × 6mm (36mm × 12mm for 1:72 model). Attach these to the inside of the engines as shown. Glue a piece of cocktail stick on the end of the strip and fix the four wheels in place.

The front undercarriage strut is made from a cocktail stick cut to 20 length (40mm for the 1:72) with the two 6mm wheels (12mm), and positioned as shown below. The drawing is half the size of the 1:144 model, one quarter of the 1:72.

Undercarriage

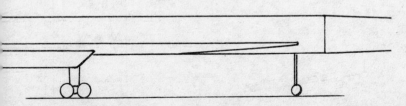

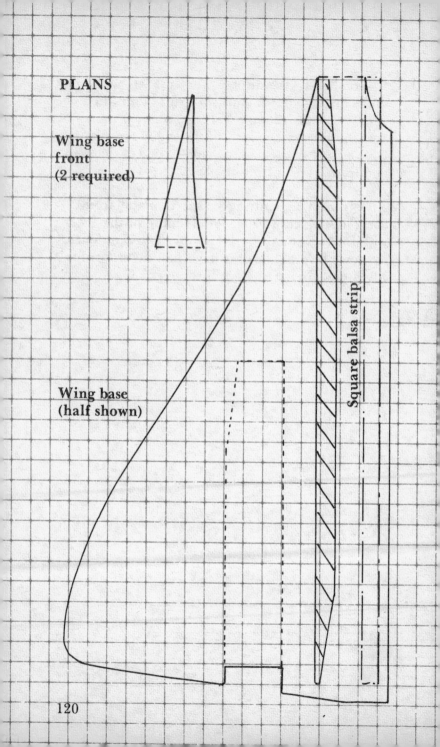

PLANS

Wing base
front
(2 required)

Wing base
(half shown)

Square balsa strip

120

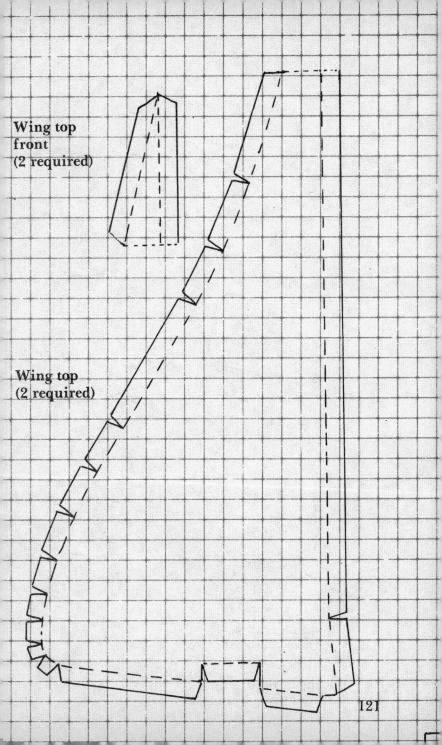

Wing top
front
(2 required)

Wing top
(2 required)

121

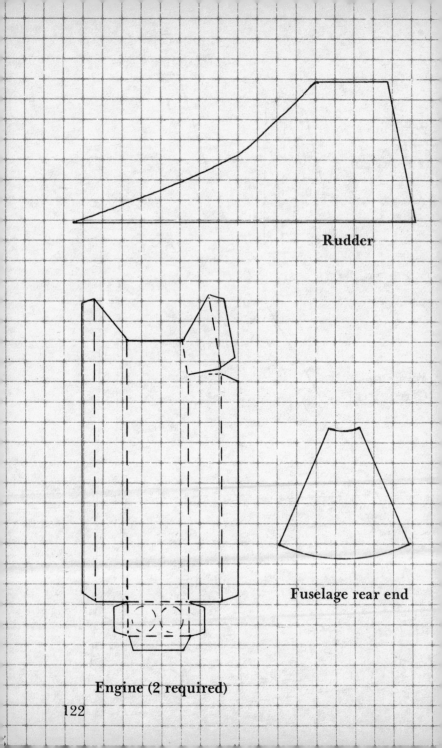

Rudder

Fuselage rear end

Engine (2 required)

122

SHUTTLE
ORBITER

SHUTTLE ORBITER

Space travel used to be all science fiction but in the last twenty years or so many of the fictional events have really happened. Men have driven a sort of beach buggy on the moon and spaceships have visited planets millions of miles away.

The Americans have now developed a re-usable space craft which could one day become the first passenger carrying spaceship. At the moment the shuttle is being developed as a transporter and mobile laboratory capable of placing satelites in orbit around the earth and then servicing them. A passenger version would probably carry about 75 people but it will be many years before space travel becomes available for all but a selected few.

Manufacturer:	The Rockwell International Corporation. U.S.A. for the National Aeronautics and Space Administration (NASA)
Power plant:	Three Rocketdyne SSME liquid Oxygen/liquid hydrogen engines
Wing span:	23.79m
Overall length:	37.26m

SHUTTLE ORBITER

Building instructions

This model, like the Concorde, can be made to 1:72 scale or 1:144 scale as given in the plans. If you wish to make the larger model, copy the plans from the 5mm grid on to a 10mm grid and follow the parts required list for the 1:72 scale.

Parts required:

1.144 scale (as plans)

5mm square balsa strip
3 jet exhausts (16mm diameter × 20mm long)
Main body – card 130mm × 100mm

1:72 scale (using 10mm grid)

10mm square balsa strip
3 jet exhausts (35mm diameter × 40mm long)
Main body-card 260mm × 200mm

For both scale models:

a)   **Stiff card**

Wing base (half shown)
Wing base front (half shown)

b) **Card**

      Wing top (2 required)
      Body rear bulkhead
      Body centre bulkhead (2 required)
      Front sides (2 required)
      Front top
      Rear side (2 required)
      Rear top
      Rudder
      Cockpit
      Engine cover (2 required)

Construction:

1. Prepare the wing base and base front from stiff card and glue or tape together. Cut the balsa strips to the length shown on the wing base plan, and shape them as shown in the shaded cross-section view. Glue the strips in position.

Wing base   **Balsa strips**

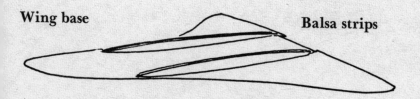

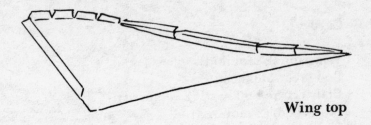

Wing top

2. Prepare the two wing tops, folding the tabs as shown.

3. Glue in place over the balsa strips and over the edge of the wing base. Fit the rear body bulkhead.

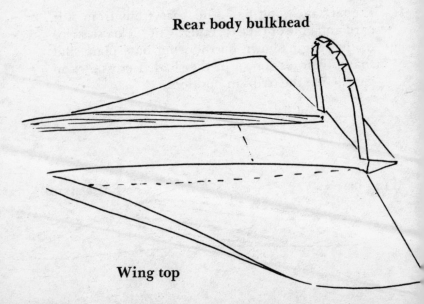

Rear body bulkhead

Wing top

4. Cut out and fit the two centre bulkheads on the dotted lines on the wing base plan, with their tabs facing outwards as shown below.

Centre bulkheads

5. Cut the oblong of card for the main body. Glue it to the tabs on the centre bulkheads and inside the wings.

Main body

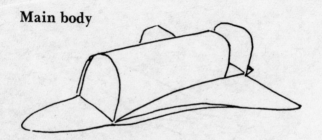

6. Fit the two rear side pieces and the rear top

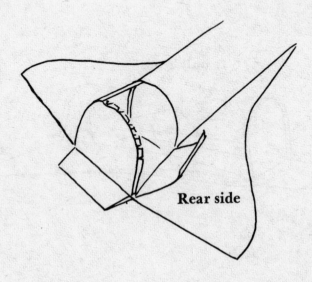

Rear side

7. Make up the rudder, folding and gluing the shaded tabs onto each other to make up the thickness.

Rudder

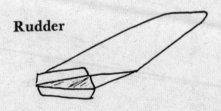

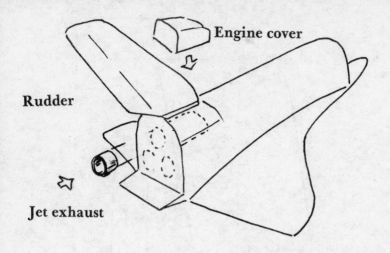

Engine cover

Rudder

Jet exhaust

8. Mount the rudder as shown. Add the two engine covers either side of the rudder and finish with the three jet exhausts.

9. Fit the two front sides and front top. Prepare the cockpit and glue in place.

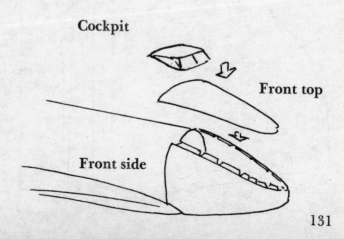

Cockpit

Front top

Front side

PLANS

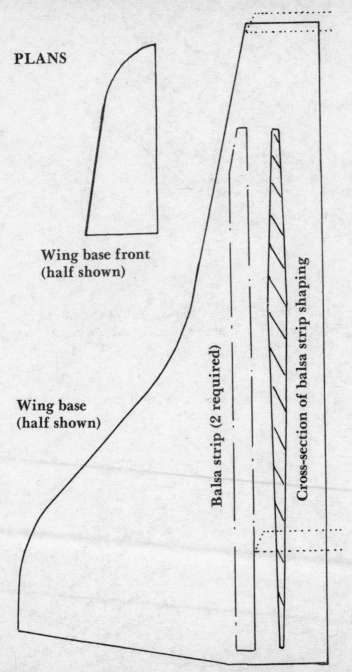

Wing base front
(half shown)

Wing base
(half shown)

Balsa strip (2 required)

Cross-section of balsa strip shaping

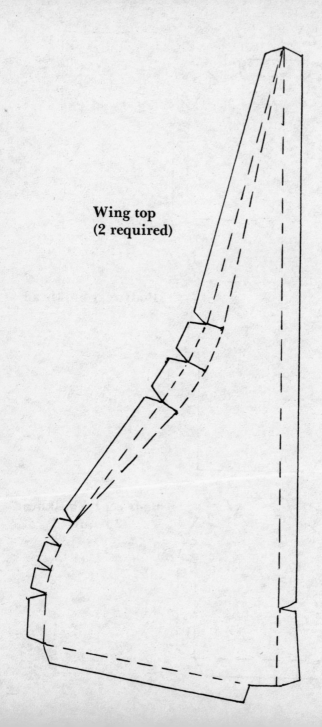

**Wing top
(2 required)**

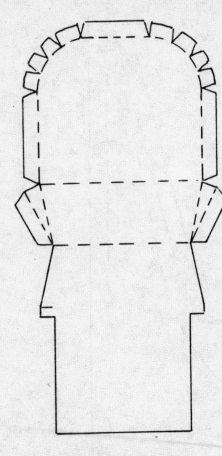

Body rear bulkhead

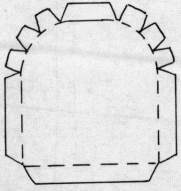

**Body centre bulkhead
(2 required)**

Front top

Front side (2 required)

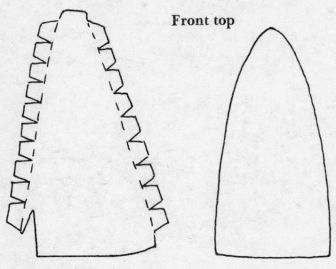

Cockpit

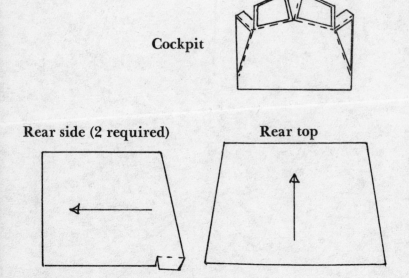

Rear side (2 required)

Rear top

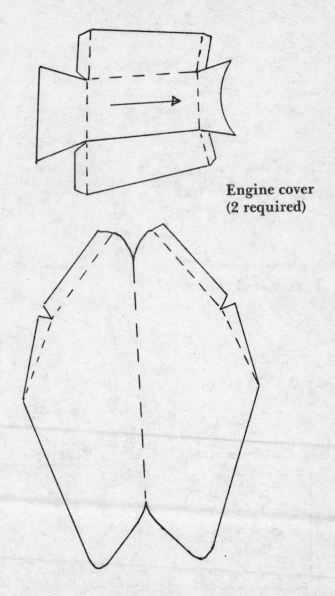

**Engine cover
(2 required)**

Rudder

MAKING MODEL RACING CARS
by Peter Fairhurst

Recreate the dazzling world of the Grand prix circuit with eight great champions representing the famous names of Formula 1 – *Tyrrell, Ferrari, Williams, McLaren – and the pre-war pioneers of racing including Mercedes, Alfa Romeo, Benz* and *E.R.A.*

These sleek, streamlined models, the most advanced and successful of their day, are simply constructed from card and balsa wood with the aid of first-rate diagrams and plans – each to perfect scale and with complete instructions for finishing and detail.

0 552 541974   85p

MAKING MODEL WARTIME VEHICLES
by Peter Fairhurst

The battlegrounds of World War II were the proving ground for many different types of wartime vehicles – from the fighting tanks and armoured cars, to the supply and service vehicles for the armed forces, mobile command and air traffic control posts, water tanks, munition carriers to name just a few.

The models you can make from this book include the *Sherman Tank* and *Fox Armoured Car,* the *German Sd KfZ II Half Track Ambulance* and a number of service vehicles including the *Matador Artillery Tractor* and the *Bedford 15cwt Mobile Canteen*.

0 552 541753   75p

MAKING MODEL CARS
by Peter Fairhurst

With a little thin card, balsa wood, glue and carbon paper, you can make thirteen exciting model cars ranging from vintage models like the *Ford Moedl T* and the *Rolls Royce Phantom II* to today's streamlined vehicles like the *Lotus Esprit,* the *Ferarri Boxer* and the *Volkswagen Golf.*

Follow the detailed plans and clear instructions and you will soon be the proud possessor of a superb fleet of cars – all to perfect scale.

0 552 541540   £1.00

WHAT CAN I DO?
by Vanessa Miles and Jacqueline Danks
Illustrated by Peter Stevenson

Do YOU know what happens behind the scenes at a television studio?

Did YOU know there is a Young Writer's Festival where YOUR play is produced?

Would YOU like to visit a hydro-electric plant?

From Steam Railways and lighthouses to craft workshops, factory visits and adventure holidays, this incredible guide contains:

Names and address of the places to visit
Leaflets and information you can send off for
Clubs you can join
Museums for different interests

AND MUCH, MUCH MORE . . . .

0 552 542504   £1.50

PRINCE PHILIP PRESENTS 101 GREAT GAMES
by Peter Heseltine and Paul James
Illustrated by Peter Stevenson

Games to play indoors; games to play outdoors; games to play on your own and games to play with friends.

Some are traditional games, some are new games but whether it is a sunny day on the beach, a birthday party at home or a rainy day that keeps you inside, you will be able to find an exciting game to amuse you and give you hours of fun and pleasure.

0 552 542466   £1.25

THE EMERGENCY HANDBOOK
by Eddie McGee
Illustrated by Rowan Barnes-Murphy

AN EMERGENCY is any happening that requires immediate action.

EMERGENCIES like: fire accidents, stings and bites, falls, poison, swimming and water accidents, nose bleeds, exposure, floods, cuts and splinters, heat exhaustion, electrocution.

THE EMERGENCY HANDBOOK tells YOU
* How to avoid them
* What to do
* Gives you a SAFETY THINK LIST for each emergency

0 552 542520   £1.20

If you would like to receive a newsletter telling you about our new children's books, fill in the coupon with your name and address and send it to:

**Gillian Osband,
Transworld Publishers Ltd.,
Century House,
61–63 Uxbridge Road, Ealing,
London, W5 5SA**

Name ....

Address ....

....

....

CHILDREN'S NEWSLETTER

All the books on the previous pages are available at your bookshop or can be ordered direct from Transworld Publishers Ltd., Cash Sales Dept., P.O. Box 11, Falmouth, Cornwall.
Please send full name and address together with cheque or postal order — no currency, and allow 22p per book to cover postage and packing (plus 10 p each for additional copies).